GEMSTONES

A TRUE BOOK

by
Ann O. Squire

Children's Press®
A Division of Scholastic Inc.

New York Toronto London Auckland Sydney
Mexico City New Delhi Hong Kong
Danbury, Connecticut

Gemstones in a market in Thailand

Reading and Content
Consultant
Jan Jenner

*Author's Dedication
To my son, Evan*

*The photograph on the cover
shows what an emerald looks
like before and after it is polished. The photograph on the
title page shows a collection
of different gemstones.*

Library of Congress Cataloging-in-Publication Data

Squire, Ann.
    Gemstones / by Ann O. Squire.
        p.   cm. – (True Books)
    Includes index.
    Summary: An introduction to gemstones, discussing the different types
of stones, where they are found, and how they are made.
    ISBN 0-516-22339-9 (lib. bdg.)   0-516-26983-6 (pbk.)
    1. Precious stones—Juvenile literature. [1. Precious stones. 2. Gems]
I. Title. II. True book.
QE392 .S784 2002
553.8—dc21   2001005756

SCHOLASTIC and associated designs are trademarks and/or registered
trademarks of Scholastic Inc. CHILDREN'S PRESS, TRUE BOOKS, and
A TRUE BOOK and all associated designs are trademarks and/or
registered trademarks of Grolier Publishing Company, Inc.
1 2 3 4 5 6 7 8 9 10 R 11 10 09 08 07 06 05 04 03 02

Contents

Members of royalty have adorned themselves with jewels for many years.

What Is a Gemstone?

Gems, such as emeralds, diamonds, and rubies, are among the rarest, most beautiful, and most valuable stones on Earth. For centuries, kings, queens, and emperors have adorned themselves with these rare treasures.

A sapphire, polished (left) and raw (right)

Gemstones are formed deep within the ground, where high heat and intense pressure transform common minerals into hard, beautiful crystals. After being cut and polished, these sparkling gems may sell for thousands of dollars.

Many gems, like ordinary rocks, are made of minerals. A mineral is a natural substance (one that is not made by humans). In addition, a mineral is always a solid. Minerals take the form of crystals, which are solids with straight edges, flat faces, and geometric shapes such as cubes or pyramids. Mineral crystals can take thousands or even

These amethyst crystals have straight, flat edges.

millions of years to grow. Most rocks are made of millions of tiny crystals packed tightly together. But a diamond or another gem is usually cut from a single, large crystal. These

large crystals can grow only
when they have enough space,
enough time, the proper tem-
perature, and the right materials.
Because of this, large, gem-
quality crystals are very rare.

These aquamarine gemstones have been cut from a larger stone and polished.

To be called a gem, a crystal must pass three tests. First, it must be rare. As we have just seen, crystals that are large enough to become gems are quite rare in the natural world.

Second, a gemstone must be beautiful. Rubies, emeralds, and sapphires are considered beautiful because of their clear, rich colors. The beauty of colorless diamonds comes from their ability to refract (bend) light, transforming it into every color of the rainbow.

Rubies (left) and sapphires (below) are the second-hardest gemstones after diamonds.

Third, a gemstone must be hard enough to last for many years without scratching or breaking. A diamond is the hardest gemstone—in fact, it is the hardest substance known. Rubies, emeralds, and sapphires are all quite hard, but they don't even come close to the diamond. In fact, diamonds are four times as hard as rubies and sapphires, the next-hardest gemstones.

Where Do Gemstones Come From?

The diamonds, rubies, and other gemstones we see today got their start millions of years ago, deep within the ground—as much as 100 miles (161 kilometers) below the surface. There the heat is so intense that even the rocks are molten (melted),

Below Earth's crust, rocks sometimes melt into magma.

forming a soft, syrupy material called magma. Scientists believe that the magma contains tiny mineral crystals that eventually become gemstones. The burning hot magma constantly pushes upward against Earth's crust. In some places the pressure is so great that the crust cracks. The magma flows upward, either breaking through the crust as an erupting volcano or flowing in between layers of rock. When this happened millions of years

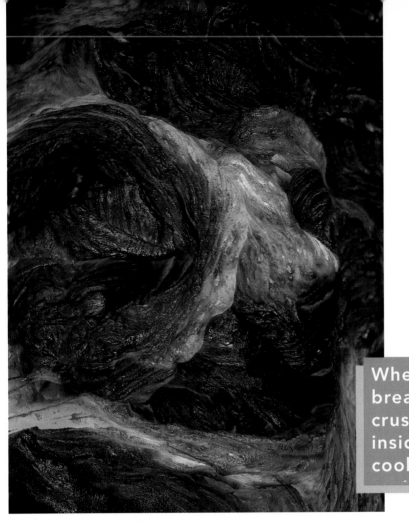

When magma breaks through the crust, the minerals inside occasionally cool to form gems.

ago, the magma slowly cooled and the mineral crystals contained within it grew and grew. Finally, gem crystals were formed.

As the years went by, the rocks surrounding the cooled magma sometimes wore away, leaving the gemstones closer to the surface, where they could be mined. Sometimes, gem-stones can now even be found *on* the earth's surface.

South Africa's diamond-mining industry began in 1867, when some children picked up a white pebble along a river bank. The "pebble" turned out to be a large and valuable diamond.

mixed in with the carbon can turn clear diamonds brown, yellow, pink, green, blue, or even black. Some of the world's most famous diamonds are colored. The 45.52-carat Hope Diamond is blue, the 137-carat Florentine Diamond is yellow, and the 41-carat Dresden Diamond is green.

Other gemstones known for their colors are rubies, sapphires, and emeralds. Amazingly, red rubies and blue sapphires are made of the same mineral compound, known as corundum. As with colored diamonds, tiny traces of different chemicals give rubies and sapphires their different colors. In the same way, the mineral called beryl can be either a grass green emerald or a pale blue aquamarine, depending on what chemical traces it contains.

Large, high-quality rubies, emeralds, and sapphires are very rare. Because of this, they can be even more valuable than diamonds.

The mineral compound corundum makes up both sapphires and rubies (above). The brilliant green color of emeralds makes them very valuable.

Tipping the Scales

A diamond's weight is calculated in carats.

Did you know that gems are weighed not in ounces or pounds, but in carats? The word carat comes from carob, a type of seed. Long ago, gem dealers weighed their stones by comparing them to the weight of a carob seed. A diamond that equaled the weight of two seeds would be a 2-carob (now called a 2-carat) diamond.

Animal, Vegetable, or Mineral?

All the gems we've discussed so far have been made of minerals. Minerals are inorganic, which means that they have never been alive. There are some gems, however, that come from organic (living) sources.

Pearls come from oysters, which are organic sources.

The most famous organic gem, the pearl, is just an oyster's way of getting out of a painful situation. Pearl oysters and pearl mussels normally rest with their shells partway open, taking in

A pearl is really a grain of sand in an oyster's shell that the animal has coated many times.

water to obtain oxygen and tiny bits of food. Sometimes a grain of sand or another object is sucked in along with the water and begins to irritate the animal's soft body. (If you've ever tried to walk with a rock in your shoe, you'll know how the oyster feels.) Having no way to get rid of the sand grain, the oyster tries to relieve its pain by covering the sharp object with layer upon layer of smooth material. This is the same material, in fact, that lines the inside of the oyster's shell. Hundreds of layers of this material, called nacre, and several years are needed to produce a medium-sized pearl.

This oyster farm produces cultivated pearls.

Natural pearls are very rare—after all, not every oyster ends up with an irritating grain of sand to deal with. So, people have figured out how to produce pearls artificially. By prying open an oyster and inserting a

These Japanese divers are searching for oysters so they can get pearls.

tiny bead, it is possible to force the oyster to make what is known as a cultured pearl. Cultured pearls look so much like natural pearls that people must use X-rays and other high-tech methods to tell the difference.

Amber and coral are also organic materials that are popular in jewelry. Amber is a brownish-yellow substance that comes from the sap of trees that lived as long as

Amber, which is hardened tree sap, is often made into jewelry.

50 million years ago. It is found on the southern coast of the Baltic Sea, Siberia, Romania, Australia, and the United States.

Coral, a pink or red material that is often carved into beads, is made from the skeletons of tiny sea creatures. The coral animal, or polyp, is soft and jellylike, with many tentacles. As it grows, a hard skeleton forms around it, and after the polyp dies, only the skeleton is left. This branching skeleton is

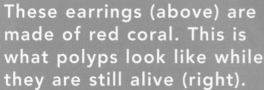

These earrings (above) are made of red coral. This is what polyps look like while they are still alive (right).

what we call coral. People in Italy and other Mediterranean countries once believed that wearing coral would protect a person against evil.

Myths and Superstitions

Nowadays, people value gemstones for their beauty and rarity, and wear them for decoration. But many years ago, people wore gemstones for different reasons. Lots of people believed that gems could be used to cure diseases. Garnets were thought

36

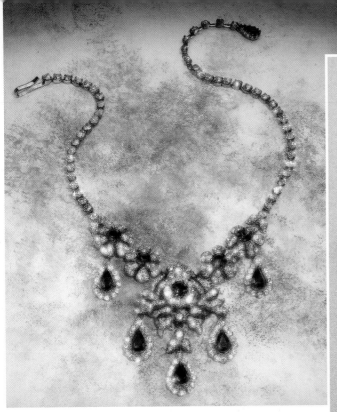

Fancy gemstones, such as in the necklace on the left, are often worn on special occasions. Long ago, garnets (right) were believed to heal fevers and depression.

to cure depression and relieve fevers. Bloodstone, a type of quartz crystal, was used to treat blood diseases. Wealthy

parents hung emeralds
around their childrens' necks
to prevent a disorder called
epilepsy. Some people even

ground emeralds to a fine powder and used them to treat eye injuries.

People also believed that gemstones had magical powers. Wearing a diamond could (supposedly) make a person strong and fearless.

Diamonds were sometimes put on crowns because it was believed that the people who wore them would be fearless.

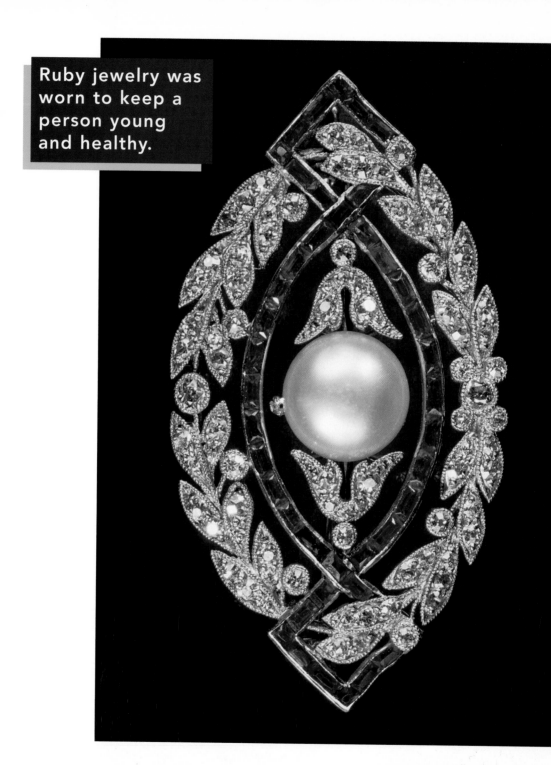

Ruby jewelry was worn to keep a person young and healthy.

Emeralds kept away witches and strengthened the memory, rubies kept a person young and healthy, and turquoise was thought to protect against injury.

It was this belief in the magical powers of gems that led to the custom of wearing birthstones. Hundreds of years ago, certain gems became linked to different months of the year. People believed that wearing the proper jewel for each month would bring good luck. Wealthy people often had twelve sets of jewelry, one for each month! But most people couldn't afford so many gems. So the custom changed, and people began wearing just the gemstone associated with their birth month.

Do You Know Your Birthstone?

Find it in the list below.

If you were born in:	Your birthstone is:
January	Garnet
February	Amethyst
March	Aquamarine or bloodstone
April	Diamond
May	Emerald
June	Pearl, moonstone, or alexandrite
July	Ruby
August	Peridot or onyx
September	Sapphire
October	Opal or tourmaline
November	Topaz or citrine
December	Turquoise or zircon

To Find Out More

Here are some additional resources to help you learn more about gemstones:

 **Books**

Davis, Gary. **Coral Reef.** Children's Press, 1997.

Downs, Sandra. **Earth's Hidden Treasures.** Twenty First Century Books, 1999.

Gallant, Roy. **Minerals.** Benchmark Books, 2000.

Hall, Cathy. **DK Handbooks: Gemstones.** DK Publications, 1994.

Harding, R.R. **Crystals and Gems.** DK Publishing, 2000.

Organizations and Online Sites

All About Jewels
http://www.allaboutjewels.com/jewel

An A-to-Z guide featuring many different jewels and gems.

Amber
http://www.emporia.edu/earthsci/amber/amber.htm

Discover different types of amber, its uses, physical properties, myths, and more.

Mineral and Gemstone Kingdom
http://www.minerals.net

A complete information guide to rocks, minerals, and gemstones. Site also includes photos and a glossary.

World of Wonder
http://www.gemsociety.org/wow/wow.htm

Information on gemology, crystals, and fun activities to learn more about gems.

Important Words

carat a unit for measuring the weight of precious stones. One carat equals 0.2 grams.

crystal a solid mineral with a geometric shape, straight edges, and smooth faces. All crystals are made up of atoms that are arranged in a regular, orderly way.

inorganic something that has never been alive. All minerals are inorganic.

magma very hot, molten rocky material that lies beneath Earth's crust.

mineral a natural, inorganic substance such as salt or gold.

molten melted

organic something that has been or is alive. Animals and plants are organic.

refract bend. Gems such as diamonds refract, or bend, the rays of light that strike them.

Index

Meet the Author

Ann O. Squire has a Ph.D. in animal behavior. Before becoming a writer, she studied African electric fish, rats, and other animals. Dr. Squire has written many books on animals, animal behavior, and other natural science topics. Her most recent books for Children's Press include *Animals of the Sea and Shore*, *African Animals*, *Animal Babies*, and *Animal Homes*. She lives with her children, Emma and Evan, in Bedford, New York.